ONLINE MEDIA INCLUDED
Audio Recordings
Printable Piano Accompaniments

PLAYBACK+
Speed • Pitch • Balance • Loop

CLASSICAL SOLOS
FOR
BARITONE
T.C.
VOLUME 2

T0071620

To access recordings and PDF accompaniments, visit:
www.halleonard.com/mylibrary

Enter Code
1129-8773-0485-4025

ISBN 978-1-70516-758-8

Visit Hal Leonard Online at
www.halleonard.com

World headquarters, contact:
Hal Leonard
7777 West Bluemound Road
Milwaukee, WI 53213
Email: info@halleonard.com

In Europe, contact:
Hal Leonard Europe Limited
1 Red Place
London, W1K 6PL
Email: info@halleonardeurope.com

In Australia, contact:
Hal Leonard Australia Pty. Ltd.
4 Lentara Court
Cheltenham, Victoria, 3192 Australia
Email: info@halleonard.com.au

LARGO
from *Xerxes*

BARITONE T.C.

GEORGE FRIDERIC HANDEL
Arranged by PHILIP SPARKE

SONGS MY MOTHER TAUGHT ME

from *Gypsy Songs*

ANTONÍN DVORÁK
Arranged by PHILIP SPARKE

BARITONE T.C.

MINUET NO. 2
from *Notebook for Anna Magdalena Bach*

BARITONE T.C.

Attributed to **CHRISTIAN PEZOLD**
Arranged by **PHILIP SPARKE**

LA CINQUANTAINE
from *Two Pieces for Cello and Piano*

JEAN GABRIEL-MARIE
Arranged by PHILIP SPARKE

BARITONE T.C.

Moderato (♩ = 80)

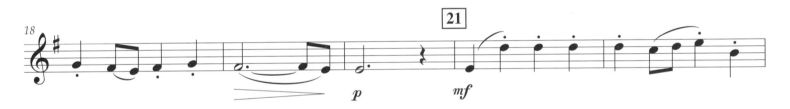

00870111

SEE, THE CONQUERING HERO COMES

from *Judas Maccabeus*

BARITONE T.C.

GEORGE FRIDERIC HANDEL
Arranged by PHILIP SPARKE

Allegro (♩ = 132)

00870111

SONATINA
Op. 36, No. 1

MUZIO CLEMENTI
Arranged by PHILIP SPARKE

BARITONE T.C.

00870111

SERENATA
from *String Quartet, Op. 3, No. 5*

BARITONE T.C.

FRANZ JOSEPH HAYDN
Arranged by PHILIP SPARKE

Andante cantabile (♩ = 96)

TAMBOURIN
from *Second Suite in E Minor*

JEAN-PHILIPPE RAMEAU
Arranged by PHILIP SPARKE

BARITONE T.C.

Vivo (♩ = 104)

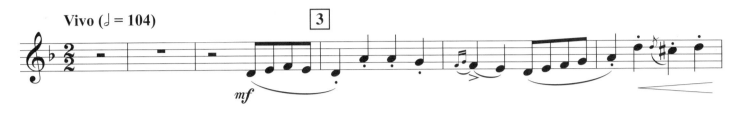

00870111

WALTZ
from *Album for the Young*

PYOTR ILYICH TCHAIKOVSKY
Arranged by PHILIP SPARKE

BARITONE T.C.

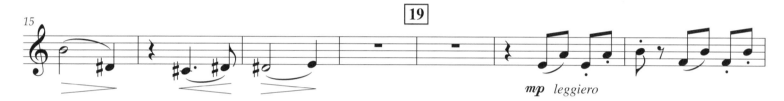

SONATINA
from *Six Pieces, Op. 3*

CARL MARIA VON WEBER
Arranged by PHILIP SPARKE

BARITONE T.C.

GAVOTTE
from *Paride ed Elena*

CHRISTOPH GLUCK/arr. JOHANNES BRAHMS
Arranged by PHILIP SPARKE

BARITONE T.C.

SONATA
Op. 118, No. 1

ROBERT SCHUMANN
Arranged by PHILIP SPARKE

BARITONE T.C.

Moderato (♩ = 104)

cresc. poco a poco

Fine

rall. (2nd time only)

D. S. al Fine

00870111

SERENADE
from *Schwanengesang, D.957*

FRANZ SCHUBERT
Arranged by PHILIP SPARKE

BARITONE T.C.

SONATINA
Anh. 5, No. 1

BARITONE T.C.

LUDWIG VAN BEETHOVEN
Arranged by PHILIP SPARKE

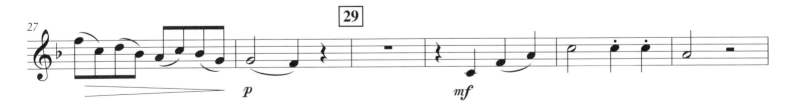

00870111

BOURRÉE
from *Flute Sonata, HWV 363b*

BARITONE T.C.

GEORGE FRIDERIC HANDEL
Arranged by PHILIP SPARKE